For Yoona, and all the other young curious minds.
It's okay to fall. You can always get back up and try again.

베라 왕
Vera Wang

분주한 뉴욕에 베라 왕이라는 이름을 가진 어린 소녀가 살았어요. 베라는 아이스 스케이트를 타는 게 너무 좋아 거의 매일 몇 시간 동안 스케이트 타는 연습을 했어요. 베라는 예쁜 옷과 음악, 멋진 동작을 좋아했고, 언젠가 아이스 스케이트 챔피언이 되는 것을 꿈꿨죠.

In bustling New York City, there was a little girl named Vera Wang. Vera enjoyed ice skating so much that she spent hours practicing almost every day. She loved the beautiful costumes, music, and graceful movements and dreamed of becoming a champion skater one day.

그런데 몇 년 동안 열심히 노력했지만, 베라는 결국 미국 올림픽 피겨 스케이트 팀에 뽑히지 못했어요. 베라는 슬펐지만, 이제 다른 것들을 해보고 또다시 좋아하는 것을 찾아야겠다고 생각했죠.

But even though she worked really hard for years, Vera couldn't make it to the U.S. Olympic figure skating team. She felt sad but knew it was time to try different things and find other passions.

대학생이 된 베라는 다른 세상이 보고 싶어 프랑스 파리에서 시간을 보내 보기로 했어요. 파리에서 베라는 수많은 다른 스타일과 아름다운 것들을 많이 보게 되었고, 곧 패션과 사랑에 빠졌어요!

When Vera was in college, she decided to spend time in Paris, France, to explore a different part of the world. In Paris, she discovered many different styles and beautiful things. Soon, she fell in love with fashion!

자연스럽게 베라는 유명 패션 잡지사에서 일을 시작하기로 결심했어요.

Naturally, Vera decided to work at a famous fashion magazine for her first job.

베라는 패션에 대한 모든 것을 배우고, 최신 트렌드에 대한 이야기를 썼죠. 창의력과 노력으로 베라는 수 백만명의 사람들이 읽는 잡지를 많이 만들었어요.

She learned all about fashion and wrote stories about the latest trends. With her creativity and hard work, she published numerous magazines that millions of people enjoyed.

베라는 자신의 일을 사랑했지만, 옷을 만들고 싶다는 꿈도 있었어요. 너무나도 사랑하는 일을 떠나는 건 쉽지 않았지만, 베라는 이제 새로운 세상을 경험할 때가 되었다고 생각했죠. 지난번처럼요.

Vera loved her job, but she aspired to create clothes, too. Although it wasn't easy to leave what she loved, she knew it was time to explore a new world, just as she had before.

그래서 베라는 큰 패션 회사에 들어갔어요.

So, she joined a big fashion company.

하지만 베라는 새로운 어려움을 겪게 되었어요. 베라는 회사의 스타일과 방향에 맞춰 생각해야 됐거든요. 베라는 자신의 생각을 마음껏 표현하고, 자신만의 아이디어를 실제로 세상에 내놓고 싶었어요.

However, Vera faced new challenges. Her imagination had to align with the company's style and direction. She craved the opportunity to fully express herself and bring her unique ideas to life.

그러던 어느 날, 결혼을 앞둔 베라는 자신에게 꼭 맞는 웨딩드레스를 찾았는데, 마음에 드는 것을 찾지 못했어요.

One day, when Vera was getting married, she searched for the perfect dress but couldn't find anything that felt right for her.

그래서 원하는 웨딩드레스를 직접 디자인하기로 결심하고, 바로 만들기 시작했죠.

So she decided to design her own dress just the way she wanted. She put her plan into action right away.

드레스는 심플하고, 우아하고, 무엇보다 중요한 건 베라에게 꼭 맞는 스타일이었어요.

The dress was simple, elegant, and most importantly, it made her feel like herself.

모두가 드레스를 좋아해서, 베라는 다른 사람들을 위해서도 아름다운 웨딩드레스를 만들어보고 싶다고 생각했죠. 베라는 두려웠지만 속으로는 알고 있었어요. 꼭 도전해 봐야 한다는 것을요.

Everyone loved it so much that Vera thought she could make beautiful wedding gowns for others too. It was definitely a scary idea, but deep inside, she knew she should give it a try.

그래서 베라는 뉴욕에 자신의 가게를 열었어요. 베라는 모든 신부들이 결혼식 날 특별하고 아름답게 느낄 수 있는 웨딩드레스를 만들고 싶었어요.
So Vera opened her own store in New York City. She wanted to create dresses that made every bride feel special and beautiful on their big day.

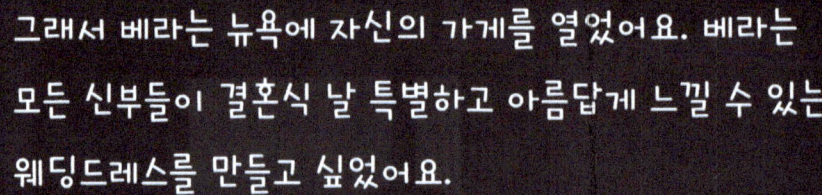

베라의 독특한 디자인은 금세 유명해져서 많은 유명인들도 베라에게 웨딩드레스를 주문하기 시작했어요.

Her unique designs quickly became so popular that many celebrities started asking her to make dresses for their weddings.

가게가 커지면서 베라는 아름다운 디자인으로 수많은 상을 받았어요. 베라의 드레스는 여러 패션 잡지, TV, 영화에 나왔죠. 재능과 노력으로 베라는 패션 아이콘이 되었어요.

As Vera's bridal shop grew, she received many awards for her stunning designs. Her dresses appeared in various fashion magazines, TV shows, and movies. Vera's talent and dedication made her a true fashion icon.

하지만 베라는 거기에서 멈추지 않았어요. 용기를 내어 안경, 향수, 일상복, 집 장식품에도 도전했죠. 베라의 작은 가게는 크고, 국제적인 브랜드가 되어 세계 많은 사람들의 사랑을 받게 되었어요.

But Vera didn't stop there. She took courage and expanded her brand to include eyewear, perfumes, ready-to-wear collections, and even home décor. Her small shop grew into a massive, international brand that many people around the world loved.

베라에게 있어서 패션은
스케이트 타는 것과 비슷했어요.
속도도 있고, 움직임도 있죠.

For Vera, fashion was very similar
to skating. There's speed, and
there's movement.

넘어지면 일어나서 다시 하면 돼요.

When you fall, you need to
get up and try again.

시간이 지나면서 베라는 이런 어려움을 받아들이고
즐겁게 헤쳐나가는 법을 배웠어요.
Over time, she learned to embrace and move
through these challenges with joy.

베라는 두려워도 괜찮다는 것을 알려주고 있어요.
중요한 건, 앞을 보고 용감하게 새로운
것들을 시도하는 거예요.

Vera taught us that it's okay to be scared.
The important thing is to look forward,
be brave, and try new things.

어떤 문이 닫히면, 언제나 다시 일어서서
새로운 문을 찾으면 되니까요.

If some doors are closed, you can always
get up and look for another door!

The Story of Vera Wang

Little Vera, the Skater

Vera Dreaming of Joining the Olympic Team

Vera's Wedding Day

Vera Wang's journey in fashion didn't happen overnight—it was built on years of hard work and a willingness to try new things. After the disappointment of not making the Olympic skating team, Vera could have given up on her dreams. Instead, she sought out new passions, and that decision changed her life.

When her first bridal designs were praised, Vera didn't stop there. She knew success wouldn't come easily, so she continued to push boundaries,

Vera's First Bridal Shop in 1990

Vera's Beautiful Dress on a TV Show

Receiving the National Medal of the Arts

expanding her work into new fields like evening gowns, perfumes, and even home décor.

Her resilience paid off, and she became one of the most famous designers in the world, known not only for her stunning creations but also for her spirit of constant growth and learning. Vera Wang's story shows that when life takes an unexpected turn, staying strong and believing in yourself can lead to extraordinary achievements.

© Copyright 2024 - Yeonsil Yoo, all rights reserved.
Paperback ISBN: 978-1-998277-53-7
Hardback ISBN: 978-1-998277-54-4

www.upflybooks.com

No part of this publication may be reproduced, stored in a retrieval system, or transmitted in any form or by any means, electronic, mechanical, photocopying, recording, or otherwise, without the prior written permission of the publisher, except as permitted under copyright law.

Photographic acknowledgments (pages 30-31):
Vera Wang's Instagram and X (@VeraWang)
Penske Media via Getty Images for Vera Wang's First Bridal Shop
Photo by Patrick Demarchelier, Vogue, June 2008, featuring Sarah Jessica Parker

Other Bilingual Korean-English Books by the Author

Get Your Next eBook for FREE! Scan the QR code or visit upflybooks.com to sign up as a beta reader!

www.ingramcontent.com/pod-product-compliance
Lightning Source LLC
Chambersburg PA
CBHW061351010526
44107CB00011B/902